This Fabulous Century 1930-1940

This booklet has been adapted and produced especially for TIME Magazine by TIME-LIFE BOOKS from the series This Fabulous Century.

Contents

© 1988 TIME-LIFE BOOKS INC.
First printing 1988. Printed in U.S.A.
Published simultaneously in Canada.

America 1930-1940

Bathing beauties at Catalina Island, California, 1933.

Radio

The cast of "Gangbusters" blasts away to open a new episode.

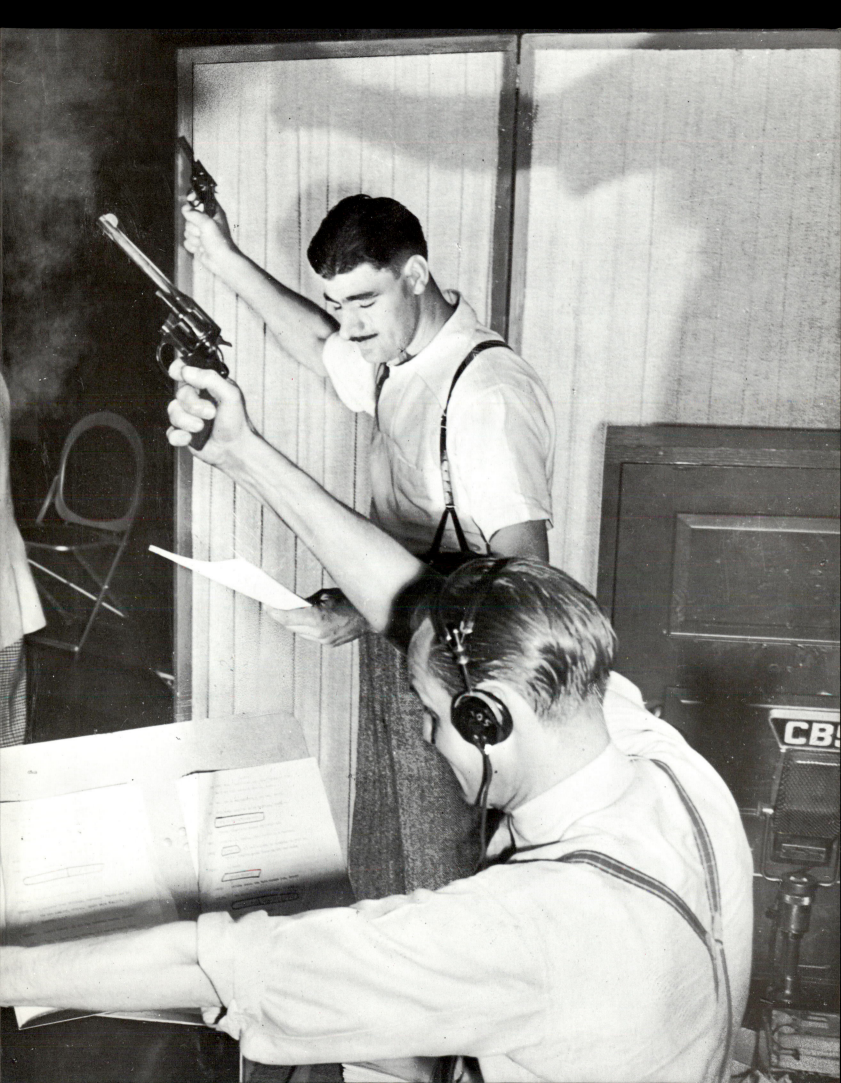

Highlights of the Six-Day Week

OZZIE NELSON AND HARRIET HILLIARD — GEORGE BURNS AND GRACIE ALLEN — FIBBER MC GEE AND MOLLY

	Sunday	Monday	Tuesday
7:00	NBC-*Red*: JELL-O PROGRAM—Jack Benny, Mary Livingstone, Kenny Baker, Don Wilson, Andy Devine, Phil Harris' orchestra NBC-*Blue*: POPULAR CLASSICS—H. Leopold Spitalny CBS: JOAN AND KERMIT—dramatic serial MBS: HAWAII CALLS	NBC-*Red*: AMOS 'N' ANDY—sketch NBC-*Blue*: MUSIC IS MY HOBBY—guests CBS: JUST ENTERTAINMENT MBS: FULTON LEWIS, JR.—Washington news commentator NBC-*Red*: UNCLE EZRA'S RADIO STATION (7:15)—Pat Barrett	NBC-*Red*: AMOS 'N' ANDY—sketch NBC-*Blue*: EASY ACES—comedy sketch CBS: JUST ENTERTAINMENT MBS: FULTON LEWIS, JR.—Washington news commentator NBC-*Blue*: MR. KEEN, TRACER OF LOST PERSONS (7:15)—dramatic serial. Bennett Kilpatrick
7:30	NBC-*Red*: INTERESTING NEIGHBORS—Jerry Belcher, interviewer NBC-*Blue*: BAKERS' BROADCAST—Feg Murray, Harriet Hilliard, Ozzie Nelson's orchestra CBS: PHIL BAKER—Beetle and Bottle, Bradley's orchestra MBS: HOLLYWOOD WHISPERS—George Fischer	NBC-*Red*: SOLOIST NBC-*Blue*: ROSE MARIE—song stylist CBS: EDDIE CANTOR'S CAMEL CARAVAN—Benny Goodman's Quartet, Bert Gordon, Walter King, Fairchild's orchestra	NBC-*Red*: BY CANDLELIGHT CBS: SECOND HUSBAND—serial, Helen Menken MBS: HEADLINES—news dramatization
8:00	NBC-*Red*: CHASE AND SANBORN PROGRAM—Don Ameche, Edgar Bergen, John Carter, Dorothy Lamour, Stroud Twins, Armbruster's orchestra NBC-*Blue*: SPY AT LARGE—dramatic serial CBS: ST. LOUIS BLUES MBS: THE WOR FORUM—S. Theodore Granik	NBC-*Red*: BURNS AND ALLEN—Tony Martin, Garber's orchestra NBC-*Blue*: RUBY NEWMAN'S ORCHESTRA CBS: YOU SAID IT!—Connie Boswell, Ted Husing, Himber's orchestra MBS: ORCHESTRA	NBC-*Red*: JOHNNY PRESENTS RUSS MORGAN AND HIS ORCHESTRA—Jack Johnstone's "Thrill of the Week" NBC-*Blue*: ENRIC MADRIGUERA AND HIS ORCHESTRA CBS: BIG TOWN—Edward G. Robinson, Claire Trevor, dramatization MBS: ORCHESTRA
8:30	NBC-*Blue*: SONGS WE REMEMBER—Gill's orchestra CBS: LYN MURRAY'S MUSICAL GAZETTE MBS: CHARIOTEERS MBS: NEWS TESTERS (8:45)—Leonard M. Leonard	NBC-*Red*: VOICE OF FIRESTONE—Richard Crooks, Margaret Speaks, Wallenstein's orchestra, guests NBC-*Blue*: THOSE WE LOVE—dramatic serial, Nan Gray, Owen Davis, Jr., Richard Cromwell, Donald Woods CBS: PICK AND PAT—comedy and music MBS: RAYMOND GRAM SWING—commentator	NBC-*Red*: LADY ESTHER SERENADE—Wayne King's orchestra NBC-*Blue*: INFORMATION PLEASE—Clifton Fadiman, John Erskine, John Kiernan and others CBS: AL JOLSON—Martha Raye, Parkyakarkus, Victor Young's orchestra, guests MBS: THE GREEN HORNET—dramatization
9:00	NBC-*Red*: MANHATTAN MERRY-GO-ROUND—Rachel Carlay, Pierre Le Kreeun, Donnie's orchestra NBC-*Blue*: HOLLYWOOD PLAYHOUSE—Tyrone Power, guests CBS: FORD SUNDAY EVENING HOUR	NBC-*Red*: MUSIC FOR MODERNS NBC-*Blue*: NOW AND THEN—orchestra CBS: LUX RADIO THEATRE—Cecil B. De Mille, guests, drama MBS: ORCHESTRA	NBC-*Red*: VOX POP—Parks Johnson, Wallace Butterworth NBC-*Blue*: HORACE HEIDT AND HIS ALEMITE BRIGADIERS—Lysbeth Hughes, Yvonne King CBS: WATCH THE FUN GO BY—Al Pearce, Nick Lucas, Hoff's orchestra MBS: ORCHESTRA
9:30	NBC-*Red*: AMERICAN ALBUM OF FAMILIAR MUSIC—Frank Munn, Jean Dickenson, Haenschen's orchestra NBC-*Blue*: JERGENS PROGRAM—Walter Winchell, news commentator MBS: ORCHESTRA NBC-*Blue*: WELCH PRESENTS IRENE RICH (9:45)—dramatization	NBC-*Red*: TALES OF GREAT RIVERS NBC-*Blue*: PAUL MARTIN AND HIS MUSIC MBS: THE WITCH'S TALE—Alonzo Deen Cole, Marie O'Flynn	NBC-*Red*: FIBBER McGEE AND MOLLY—Jim Jordan, Clark Dennis, Betty Winkler, Mills' orchestra NBC-*Blue*: NBC JAMBOREE—Don McNeill, Sylvia Clark, Fran Allison, Little Jackie Heller, Bill Thompson CBS: BENNY GOODMAN'S SWING SCHOOL MBS: MUSIC BY—guest artists
10:00	NBC-*Red*: HOUR OF CHARM—Phil Spitalny's All Girl orchestra NBC-*Blue*: NORMAN CLOTIER'S ORCHESTRA CBS: GRAND CENTRAL STATION—dramatic sketch	NBC-*Red*: CONTENTED PROGRAM—Opal Craven, Marek Weber's orchestra NBC-*Blue*: MAGNOLIA BLOSSOMS—Fisk Jubilee Choir CBS: WAYNE KING'S ORCHESTRA	NBC-*Red*: BELIEVE IT OR NOT—Robert L. Ripley, Rolfe's orchestra CBS: TIME TO SHINE—Hal Kemp's orchestra, Judy Starr, Bob Allen
10:30	NBC-*Red*: SYMPHONIC VARIATIONS—Walter Logan's orchestra NBC-*Blue*: CHEERIO—talk and music CBS: HEADLINES AND BYLINES—H. V. Kaltenborn, Bob Trout, Erwin Canham—news commentators	NBC-*Red*: FOR MEN ONLY NBC-*Blue*: NATIONAL RADIO FORUM—guest speaker CBS: LET FREEDOM RING—dramatizations MBS: HENRY WEBER'S PAGEANT OF MELODY	NBC-*Red*: JIMMIE FIDLER'S HOLLYWOOD GOSSIP CBS: RAY HEATHERTON—songs MBS: ORCHESTRA NBC-*Red*: DALE CARNEGIE (10:45)—How To Win Friends and Influence People
11:00	NBC-*Red*: DANCE MUSIC NBC-*Blue*: PRESS-RADIO NEWS; ORCHESTRA CBS: ORCHESTRA MBS: ORCHESTRA	NETWORK SIGN OFF (Local programming only)	NBC-*Red*: DANCE MUSIC NBC-*Blue*: DANCE MUSIC CBS: DANCE MUSIC MBS: DEVELOPMENT OF MUSIC

As this schedule for the week of June 5, 1938, indicates, the big evening shows of radio's week ran from Sunday through Friday on four networks (two

| Wednesday | KAY KYSER | Thursday | MAJOR BOWES | Friday | MR. FIRST NIGHTER |

Wednesday	Thursday	Friday
NBC–*Red*: AMOS 'N' ANDY—sketch NBC–*Blue*: EASY ACES—comedy sketch NBC–*Red*: UNCLE EZRA'S RADIO STATION (7:15)— Pat Barrett NBC–*Blue*: MR. KEEN, TRACER OF LOST PERSONS (7:15)— dramatic serial, Bennett Kilpatrick	NBC–*Red*: AMOS 'N' ANDY—sketch NBC–*Blue*: EASY ACES—comedy sketch NBC–*Blue*: MR. KEEN, TRACER OF LOST PERSONS (7:15)— dramatic serial CBS: HOLLYWOOD SCREEN SCOOPS (7:15)— George McCall MBS: OUTDOORS WITH BOB EDGE (7:15)	NBC–*Red*: AMOS 'N' ANDY—sketch NBC–*Blue*: THE FOUR OF US CBS: JUST ENTERTAINMENT MBS: FULTON LEWIS, JR.—Washington news commentator NBC–*Blue*: STORY BEHIND THE HEADLINES (7:15)— Cesar Saerchinger
NBC–*Red*: TALES BY EDWIN C. HILL NBC–*Blue*: ROSE MARIE—song stylist NBC–*Red*: HAPPY JACK (7:45)—songs NBC–*Blue*: SCIENCE ON THE MARCH (7:45) CBS: HISTORY'S HEADLINES (7:45)	NBC–*Red*: VOCALIST NBC–*Blue*: VOCALIST CBS: ST. LOUIS BLUES MBS: HEADLINES—news dramatization	NBC–*Blue*: TALES OF EDWIN C. HILL CBS: VOCALIST NBC–*Red*: THREE ROMEOS (7:45) NBC–*Blue*: VOCALIST (7:45) CBS: SCIENCE AND SOCIETY (7:45)
NBC–*Red*: ONE MAN'S FAMILY—sketch NBC–*Blue*: ROY SHIELD'S REVUE CBS: CAVALCADE OF AMERICA—guests, Voorhees' orchestra MBS: ORCHESTRA	NBC–*Red*: ROYAL GELATIN PROGRAM—Rudy Vallee, guests NBC–*Blue*: MARCH OF TIME—news dramatizations CBS: KATE SMITH—Ted Collins, Miller's orchestra MBS: ALFRED WALLENSTEIN'S SINFONIETTA	NBC–*Red*: CITIES SERVICE CONCERT—Lucille Manners, Frank Black's orchestra NBC–*Blue*: MAURICE SPITALNY'S ORCHESTRA CBS: THE GHOST OF BENJAMIN SWEET— dramatic serial
NBC–*Red*: RALEIGH AND KOOL SHOW—Tommy Dorsey's orchestra, Edythe Wright, Jack Leonard, Paul Stewart NBC–*Blue*: HARRIET PARSONS—Hollywood commentator CBS: BEN BERNIE—Lew Lehr, Buddy Clark MBS: LET'S VISIT—Dave Driscoll, Jerry Danzig	MBS: THE GREEN HORNET—dramatization NBC–*Blue*: PIANO DUO (8:45)	NBC–*Blue*: DEATH VALLEY DAYS—dramatization CBS: PAUL WHITEMAN'S ORCHESTRA—Joan Edwards MBS: TOPICS OF THE DAY—speaker
NBC–*Red*: TOWN HALL TONIGHT—Fred Allen, Portland Hoffa, Van Steeden's orchestra NBC–*Blue*: TUNE TYPES—variety program CBS: ANDRE KOSTELANETZ—Deems Taylor, guests MBS: ORCHESTRA MBS: JOHNSON FAMILY (9:15)—sketch, with Jimmy Scribner	NBC–*Red*: GOOD NEWS OF 1938—Robert Taylor, Fannie Brice, Frank Morgan, Willson's orchestra NBC–*Blue*: TORONTO PROMENADE CONCERT CBS: MAJOR BOWES' AMATEUR HOUR MBS: THE HARMONAIRES	NBC–*Red*: WALTZ TIME—Frank Munn, Lyman's orchestra NBC–*Blue*: ROYAL CROWN REVUE—Tim and Irene, Uncle Happy, Graham McNamee, Fredda Gibson, George Olsen's orchestra CBS: HOLLYWOOD HOTEL—Louella Parsons, Frances Langford, Frank Parker, Ken Murray MBS: ORCHESTRA
NBC–*Blue*: BOSTON "POP" CONCERT CBS: THE WORD GAME—Max Eastman MBS: JAZZ NOCTURNE—Helene Daniels, Stanley's orchestra	MBS: RAY SINATRA'S MOONLIGHT RHYTHMS— Sylvia Froos, Jack Arthur	NBC–*Red*: A. L. ALEXANDER'S TRUE STORIES— dramatization NBC–*Blue*: NBC SPELLING BEE—Paul Wing MBS: WLW OPERETTA
NBC–*Red*: KAY KYSER'S MUSICAL CLASS AND DANCE NBC–*Blue*: CHOIR SYMPHONETTE CBS: GANGBUSTERS—crime dramatizations, Col. H. Norman Schwartzkopf MBS: ORCHESTRA	NBC–*Red*: KRAFT MUSIC HALL—Bing Crosby, Bob Burns, Trotter's orchestra, guests NBC–*Blue*: UNDER WESTERN SKIES CBS: ESSAYS IN MUSIC—Victor Bay's orchestra, Margaret Daum, Ruth Carhart, David Ross MBS: DRAMATIZATION	NBC–*Red*: FIRST NIGHTER—dramatization, Les Tremayne, Barbara Luddy NBC–*Blue*: PAUL MARTIN'S ORCHESTRA CBS: COLUMBIA SQUARE MBS: BAMBERGER SYMPHONY ORCHESTRA
NBC–*Blue*: NBC MINSTREL SHOW—Gene Arnold, orchestra CBS: EDGAR GUEST IN "IT CAN BE DONE"— Marion Francis Masters' orchestra MBS: MELODIES FROM THE SKY	NBC–*Blue*: NBC PROMENADE CONCERT CBS: AMERICANS AT WORK MBS: HENRY WEBER'S CONCERT REVUE	NBC–*Red*: JIMMIE FIDLER'S HOLLYWOOD GOSSIP MBS: CURTAIN TIME—dramatization CBS: AMERICAN VIEWPOINT (10:45)
NBC–*Red*: DANCE MUSIC NBC–*Blue*: DANCE MUSIC CBS: DANCE MUSIC MBS: ORCHESTRA	NBC–*Red*: SPORTS QUESTION BOX NBC–*Blue*: ORCHESTRA CBS: DUKE ELLINGTON'S ORCHESTRA NBC–*Blue*: ELZA SCHALLERT REVIEWS (11:15)— previews, guests MBS: THEATRE DIGEST (11:15)	NBC–*Red*: DANCE MUSIC NBC–*Blue*: ORCHESTRA CBS: DANCE MUSIC MBS: DANCE MUSIC

belonged to NBC and were code-named Red and Blue). Saturday night most people went to the movies; a few stayed home to hear "Your Hit Parade."

Hard Times

Shacks of Seattle's Hooverville shelter the homeless.

The Face of Poverty

Before daylight we were on the way to Chevrolet. The police were
already on the job, waving us away from the office.
"Nothin' doin'. Nothin' doin'." Now we were tramping through
falling snow. Dodge employment office. A big
well fed man in a heavy overcoat stood at the door saying, "No, no,"
as we passed before him. On the tramp again. . . .

AN UNEMPLOYED DETROIT AUTO WORKER

Desperate for work, a Detroiter advertises. Others bought jobs; one man paid a $10 fee to earn $13.50.

Jobless New Yorkers haunt the employment agencies on Sixth Avenue. One agency averaged 5,000 applicants daily—and had work for only 300.

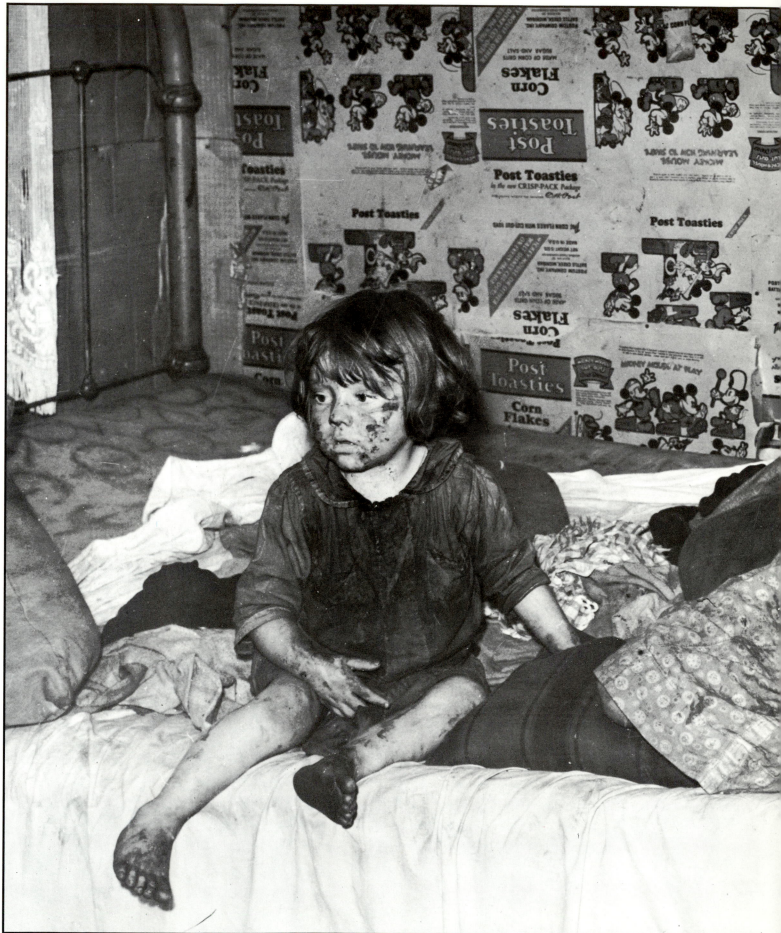

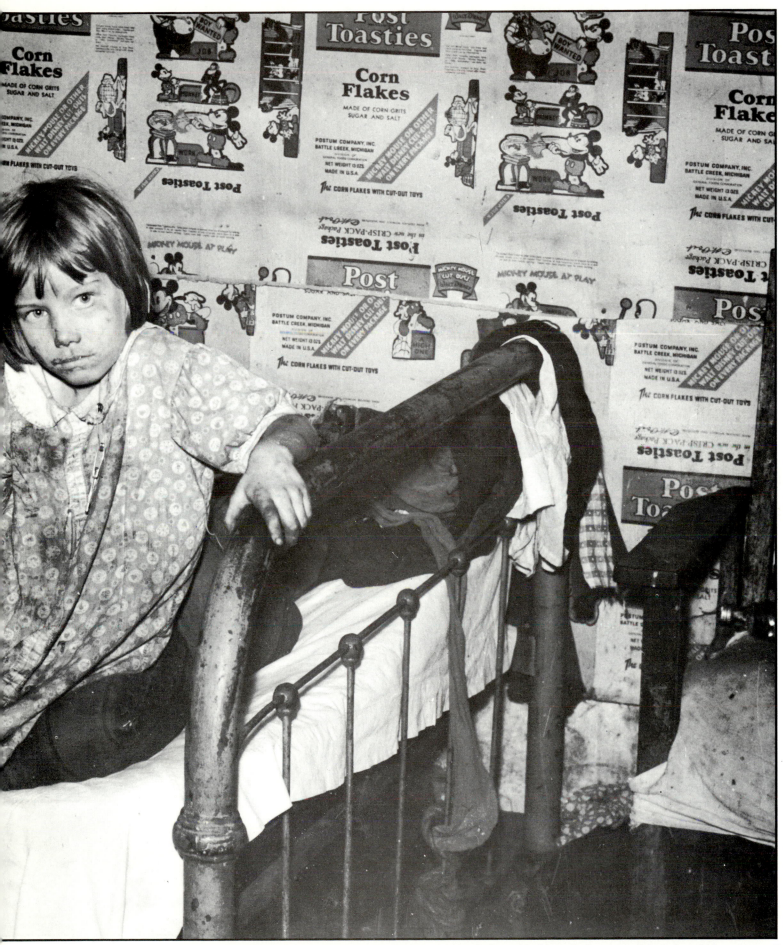

The daughters of a WPA worker and a sick mother are left home unattended. A bitter father said: "A worker's got no right to have kids any more."

An abandoned farm lies inundated by dust. Departing farmers reduced the population of Hall County, Texas, from 14,392 to only 7,000.

All that dust made some of the
farmers leave; they became the Okies. We stuck
it out here. We scratched, literally
scratched, to live. We'd come to town to sell
sour cream for nine cents
a pound. If we could find a town big
enough and far enough away
from the dust, we could sell eggs at ten cents
a dozen. Despite all the dust
and the wind, we were putting in crops, but
making no crops and barely
living out of barnyard products only. We
made five crop failures in five years.

AN OKLAHOMA FARMER

"For Sale" signs marked the start of the dust bowlers' migrations.

15

October-December 1932. Cut Malaga and muscat grapes
near Fresno. About $40 a month.
December 1932. Left for Imperial Valley, Calif.
February 1933. Picked peas, Imperial Valley. Earned $30 for season.
On account of weather, was fortunate to break even.
March-April 1933. Left for Chicago. Returned to California.
May 1933. Odd jobs on lawns and radios at Fresno.
June 1933. Picked figs near Fresno. Earned $50 in two months.

A MIGRATORY WORKER'S LOG BOOK

Rude cardboard shacks served as winter quarters for migrants in California's Imperial Valley.

A large family, intact despite its migrations, gathers to share a simple meal. "Us people has got to stick together to get by these hard times."

17

The Company of Heroes

Leapin' Lizards! Who says business is bad?
LITTLE ORPHAN ANNIE, 1933

During the '30s, the world of little kids orbited around a set of heroes and heroines whose extravagant lives were chronicled in a rich new range of media. Every Sunday before church, kids all over the country pawed through the funny papers for the latest exploits of Flash Gordon or Little Orphan Annie, whose pet expression "Leapin' Lizards!" was an American standard and whose faith in good old capitalism comforted many a Depression-ridden parent. On weekdays Annie also came booming over the radio, joined by the likes of hard-bitten detective Dick Tracy and Jack Armstrong, a teen-age football hero. Saturday was movie day: four and a half raucous hours of cliff-hanging serials featuring Tarzan or Flash Gordon, animated cartoons, and then perhaps a full-length picture starring that all-time heroine, Shirley Temple. In between times, the kids caught up on back adventures of the same characters through Big Little Books—squat, 400-page cubes of type and pictures that sold for a dime—or amused themselves with pop-up and cut-out books of Shirley, Buck Rogers or a pair of overseas idols, Princesses Elizabeth and Margaret Rose of England.

The kingdoms of these heroes and heroines were even more varied than the media that brought them home to the kids; they ranged from America's playing fields to the slimiest Oriental jungles, from the plains of the Old West to the slums of gangster-ridden cities, from Buckingham Palace to galaxies in the far reaches of outer space. And the idols themselves were just as varied in their makeup; some were real (the Little Princesses), some wholly fabricated (Buck Rogers), others physically real but fictitious in their exploits (Tom Mix and Shirley Temple).

The common ground on which these heroes and heroines stood was virtue, a commodity they sold in heaping portions by proving that good, clean living held unlimited rewards. With the exception of the Little Princesses, the idols also proved awesomely adept at selling commercial products. With each installment of their adventures, they unblushingly fired off a barrage of sales pitches in behalf of various trinkets, toys and breakfast foods. Little Orphan Annie even managed to pitch a chocolate drink called Ovaltine with her left hand while handing out her conservative, pro-business dogma with the right. Despite such blatant salesmanship, however, the most successful product served up by the kids' idols was an inexpensive and wonderful world of make-believe, during hard times when the real world often seemed to be no fun at all.

Moppets, carefully coiffed and rehearsed by would-be movie mothers, participate in a Shirley Temple look-alike contest in Herrin, Illinois.

Little Orphan Annie

When Little Orphan Annie first appeared, she seemed out of place on the funny pages, for the simple reason that she was rarely funny. Rather, cartoonist Harold Gray time and again rallied his never-aging red-haired tyke and her mongrel Sandy to the aid of decent folks who were cowering before treacherous foreigners, mortgage-holders and crimelords. Often Annie's wealthy foster father, Oliver "Daddy" Warbucks, would happen by with his homicidal henchmen Punjab and The Asp to give Annie a hand.

Launched in 1924, the strip's success soon affected *Annie's* story line. Gray, who by 1934 was earning about $100,000 a year, began to color the melodrama with his conservative views on labor leaders and liberal politicians. Only when Annie went on radio did Gray compromise his —and the orphan's—philosophy of "ya hafta earn what ya get"; Annie gave away a glittering array of premiums in exchange for seals from the jars of sponsor Ovaltine's chocolate milk mix. However, $1,000 a week soothed Gray's anguish at the thought of all those free rings, badges, shake-up mugs and those secret-code cards *(right)* that allowed Annie's radio followers to decode such momentous messages as: 8-36-18-28-22/30-44-2-24-40-18-28-10.

ANNIE RINGS

BUTTONS

SHAKE-UP MUG

SECRET SOCIETY BADGES AND CODE

BRACELETS

Little Orphan Annie's Song

Who's that little chatterbox?
The one with pretty auburn locks?
Who do you see?
It's Little Orphan Annie....

Bright eyes, cheeks a rosy glow,
There's a store of healthiness handy.
Mite-size, always on the go.
And if you want to know—"Arf!" says Sandy....

COMIC BOOK PREMIUM

MEMBERSHIP OATH

MEMBERSHIP SONG

AUTOGRAPHED PHOTO OF TONY AND TOM

Tom Mix

"Reach for the sky! Lawbreakers always lose, Straight Shooters always win!! It pays to shoot straight!!!" Young radio listeners thrilled to hear cowboy character Tom Mix bark out this instructive battle cry. Naturally, when their hero commanded them to eat his sponsor Ralston's wheat cereal, they hastened to do so; and when Tom said that a few Ralston box tops would yield the treasures shown here, what real Straight Shooter could resist?

Tom's radio fans had plenty of company in their worship of the hard-jawed idol. Long before the radio show began in 1933, Mix had built up an international following

that had rooted for him and the Wonder Horse Tony through some 180 feature films.

In real life, the old Straight Shooter was an old roué who ran through three wives and four million dollars. Nevertheless he guarded his public image as a nonsmoking teetotaler. "I want to keep my pictures in such a vein that parents will not object to letting their children see me on the screen," explained Tom solemnly. And all his fans believed him, remaining loyal literally to the end: when he died in 1940, the Tom Mix Club of Lisbon, Portugal, gave up movies for two weeks as a sign of mourning.

SLIDE-WHISTLE RING

SIREN RING

MAGNET RING

MIRROR RING

CLUB RING

HORSESHOE NAIL RING

SIGNATURE RING

COMPASS AND MAGNIFIER

CLUB BADGE

WRANGLER BADGE

DECODER BADGE

COWBOY SPUR

TOY SIX-SHOOTER

POCKETKNIFE

FLASHLIGHT

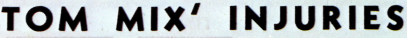

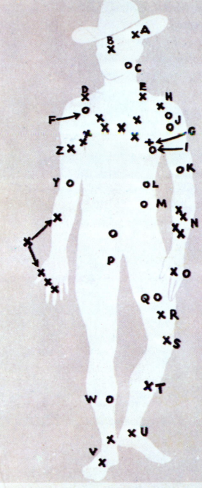

TOM MIX' INJURIES

Danger and difficulty have never daunted Tom Mix, nor broken bones stopped him. He has been blown up once, shot 12 times and injured 47 times in movie stunting. The chart shows the location of some of Tom's injuries. (X marks fractures; circles, bullet wounds.)

A. Skull fractured in accident.
B. Nose injured when artillery wagon blew up in China.
C. Shot thru jaw by sniper in Spanish-American War.
D. Shoulder fractured in circus accident.
E. Collar bone broken four times in falls.
F. Shot by bandit in Mix home.
G. Eight broken ribs from movie accidents.
H. Shoulder fractured when horse was shot from under him by bandits in U. S. Marshal days.
I. Shot by cattle rustlers in Texas.
J. Shot twice in left arm by Oklahoma outlaws.
K. Shot below elbow by outlaw.
L. Shot through abdomen by killer he arrested.
M. Wounded in gun fight with rustlers.
N. Left arm broken four times in movie stunting.
O. Hand broken in movie stunt.
P. Shot by bad man while Oklahoma sheriff.
Q. Shot in leg when 14 years old.
R. Leg trampled by horse.
S. Fractured knee in wagon accident.
T. Leg broken while stunting for movies.
U. Fractured ankle breaking wild horses.
V. Foot and ankle broken in wagon accident.
W. Shot through leg by bank robbers.
X. Three broken fingers, hand and arm fractured in screen fights and film stunting.
Y. Shot through elbow in real stage coach hold-up (1902).
Z. Broken arm in film stunting.

NOTE: Scars from twenty-two knife wounds are not indicated, nor is it possible to show on the diagram the hole four inches square and many inches deep that was blown in Tom's back by a dynamite explosion.

The Daredevil Crooks

The criminal army in America today is on the march. . . . Crime is today sapping the spiritual and moral strength of America.

J. EDGAR HOOVER

Johnnie's just an ordinary fellow. Of course, he goes out and holds up banks and things, but he's really just like any other fellow, aside from that.

A FRIEND OF JOHN DILLINGER

Hard times brought a marked boom for at least one profession—crime. While legitimate businesses closed and farms lay barren, an alarming number of Americans began looking for easy money through robbery, kidnaping and even murder. Across the Midwest, bands of marauders traveling in fast-moving cars and toting sawed-off shotguns and Tommy guns began knocking over rural banks and Post Offices. In large cities, tightly organized undergrounds were raking in millions of dollars through extortion, prostitution and auto theft rings. By 1935, according to one estimate by the Justice Department, so many Americans had moved to the shady side of the law that crooks outnumbered carpenters by four to one, grocers by six to one and doctors by 20 to one.

The first of the decade's lawbreakers to win real notoriety, and surely the most hated criminal of his time, was an ex-convict from Germany named Bruno Richard Hauptmann. On the night of March 1, 1932, Hauptmann climbed up to a second-story nursery bedroom in Hopewell, New Jersey, and kidnaped the 20-month-old son of aviation hero Charles Lindbergh. The nation was stunned. It was as though Hauptmann had violated every home in America. For Lindy was the country's favorite hero, a modest, tousled-haired symbol of American courage and integrity. Though Lindy paid $50,000 in ransom, the baby was found dead six weeks later, and when Hauptmann was finally caught and executed in the electric chair, the country registered deep satisfaction.

But the country had some strikingly different feelings about other crimes and criminals; many people, impoverished and embittered by the Depression, actually found a certain justice in the mounting number of bank robberies. The most notorious of the bank thieves, John Dillinger, even emerged as a kind of Robin Hood folk hero. "Dillinger did not rob poor people. He robbed those who became rich by robbing the poor," wrote an admirer in Indianapolis. "I am for Johnnie." Indeed, Dillinger projected an image of swashbuckling glamor and generosity. When holding up a bank he would leap the barrier to the teller's cage to grab the loot. Once, when he broke out with two hostages from a supposedly escape-proof Indiana jail, he gave the men four dollars carfare home. In their admiration Dillinger's fans managed to forget that their hero had gunned down 10 men during his career, and that—like the other bandits shown on the following pages—he was basically just a cold-blooded thug.

America's No. 1 desperado, John Dillinger, smiles while he shows off some of the tools of his trade: a Thompson submachine gun and a pistol.

Key members of the Barker gang included "Dock" (top left), Freddie and "Ma", shown with boyfriend Arthur Dunlop.

"Ma" Barker and Her Boys

Arizona Clark "Ma" Barker, who believed in crime for the whole family, reared her four sons to be God-fearing, obedient thugs. Each Sunday she dragged them off to church; weekdays she schooled them in the finer points of thievery, kidnaping and murder. The Barkers shown here, joined by brothers Herman and Lloyd—and occasionally by other gangland luminaries—pulled off so many audacious capers, that they became the all-time leaders in major crime, family style.

WANTED FOR MURDER
JOPLIN, MISSOURI

F.P.C.29 - MO. 9
26 U 00 6

CLYDE CHAMPION BARROW, age 24, 5'7", 130#, hair dark brown and
wavy, eyes hazel, light complexion, home West Dallas, Texas.
This man killed Detective Harry McGinnis and Constable
J.W. Harryman in this city, April 13, 1933.

BONNIE PARKER   CLYDE BARROW   CLYDE BARROW

This man is dangerous and is known to have committed the following
murders: Howard Hall, Sherman, Texas; J.N.Bucher, Hillsboro, Texas;
a deputy sheriff at Atoka, Okla; deputy sheriff at West Dallas,
Texas; also a man at Belden, Texas.
        The above photos are kodaks taken by Barrow and his com-
panions in various poses, and we believe they are better for
identification than regular police pictures.
        Wire or write any information to the

                                        Police Department.

The Barrow gang's fondness for hamming in front of a Kodak made identification easier for pursuing lawmen.

Bonnie and Clyde

The most sadistic of the decade's hoods, Clyde Barrow shot down people for the sheer love of killing. He embarked on a murder-and-robbery spree through Missouri, Texas and Oklahoma with his moll, cigar-chomping Bonnie Parker, and a succession of young men. Ill-tempered and somewhat effeminate, Barrow was generally despised by other Midwestern bandits, who felt that his haphazard killings and frequently bungled robberies lowered the standards of the profession.

That Man in the White House

Never was there such a change in the transfer of a government. The President is the boss, the dynamo, the works.   ARTHUR KROCK IN *THE NEW YORK TIMES*, MARCH 12, 1933

When Franklin D. Roosevelt became the 32nd President of the United States, the country was scared, more scared than ever in its history. That very morning, March 4, 1933, every last bank in the nation had had to close its doors. The old leaders were ashen-faced. "I'm afraid," said the chairman of Bethlehem Steel, Charles Schwab, "every man is afraid."

On the high inaugural platform in front of the Capitol, the 51-year-old President-elect repeated the oath of office in a clear, deliberate voice, looked out over the tense throng covering 10 acres of lawn and pavement and said: "This Nation asks for action, and action now." Entering his car to go to the White House, he clasped his strong hands over his head in the salute of a champion. The next morning, rolling in a wheelchair as he had since he was crippled by polio 12 years before, Roosevelt moved into the oval office of Presidents. He sat alone for a few moments, then gave a great shout for his aides and began to act, starting with a call for a special session of Congress. His emergency banking bill strengthening the nation's financial system roared through the House unchanged in 38 minutes. When the banks reopened four days later, deposits exceeded withdrawals. The immediate panic was over. The nation's confidence was beginning to return.

Sensing opportunity, F.D.R. kept the lawmakers in session. In the next 100 days, riding herd on the uneasy nation with a firmer rein than it had felt since the days of his cousin, Teddy Roosevelt, he permanently altered the conduct of American life. Fifteen major messages streamed from the White House to Capitol Hill. When Congress adjourned on June 16, fifteen new laws assured concerted government action: to employ the jobless, to develop the backward Tennessee Valley, to support crop prices, to repeal Prohibition, to stop home foreclosures, to insure bank deposits, to stabilize the economy, and more.

F.D.R. called the program a "New Deal" for the nation, but others thought it went beyond that. "We have had our revolution," said *Collier's* magazine. "We like it." The people raised their heads; even the well-to-do were at first delighted. As Roosevelt had noted, action, any kind of action, had been their plea. Kansas' Republican governor, Alf Landon, had said: "Even the iron hand of a dictator is in preference to a paralytic stroke." Now industrialist Pierre du Pont sent F.D.R. a friendly letter. And press lord William Randolph Hearst flattered F.D.R.: "I guess at your next election we will make it unanimous."

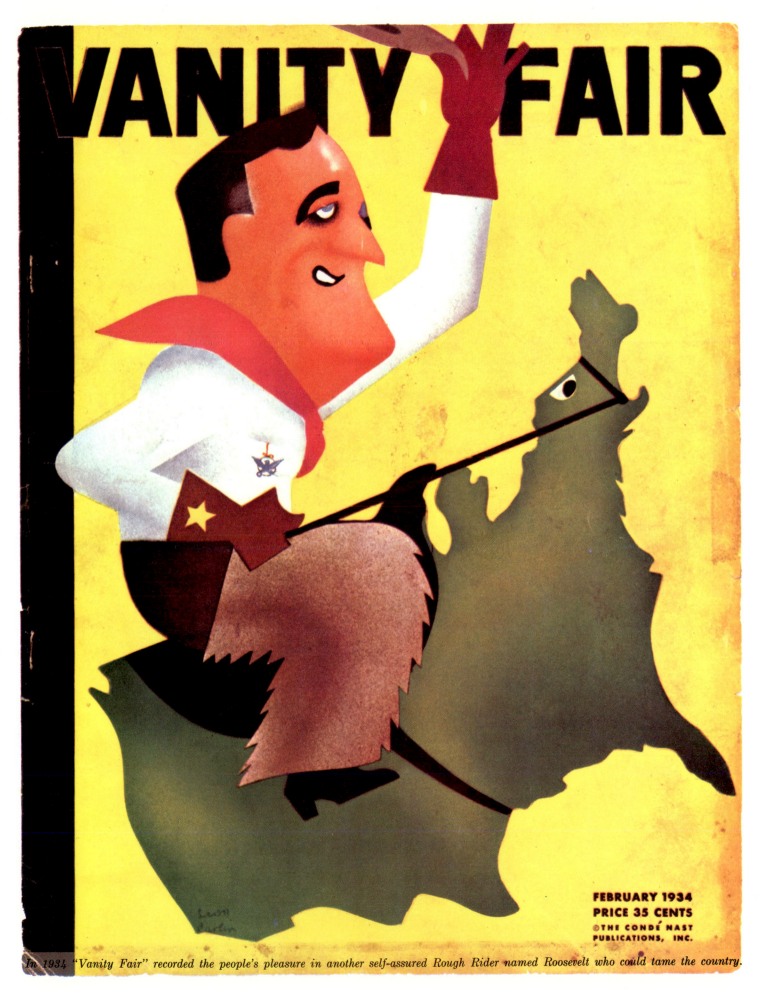

VANITY FAIR

FEBRUARY 1934
PRICE 35 CENTS
©THE CONDÉ NAST
PUBLICATIONS, INC.

In 1934 "Vanity Fair" recorded the people's pleasure in another self-assured Rough Rider named Roosevelt who could tame the country.

F.D.R. and his wife, Eleanor, were both energetic, strong-willed and independent. She believed he might have been happier with a less critical wife.

The Look of the New Family

The second family of Roosevelts to move into the White House within a quarter century was an exciting batch of individualists with lots of verve and offspring *(below)*. Each of F.D.R.'s children tended to go his own way, but Christmas Eve always found the clan gathered. Surrounded by grandchildren, F.D.R. read from Dickens' *A Christmas Carol*, acting out the parts of Scrooge and Tiny Tim with gusto. Next day, at Christmas dinner, he carved paper-thin slices of turkey, boasting "You can almost *read* through it." As the Presidency wore on, however, Roosevelt had less and less time for family matters. One day when a distraught son poured out his troubles, F.D.R. absently handed him a paper, saying: "This is a most important document—I should like to have your opinion on it."

A Spreading Tree

ANNA   JAMES   ELLIOTT   FRANKLIN JR.   JOHN

CURTIS DALL   JOHN BOETTIGER   BETSY CUSHING   ELIZABETH DONNER   RUTH GOOGINS   ETHEL DU PONT   ANNE CLARK

SISTIE   JOHN   SARA   WILLIAM   RUTH   FRANKLIN III

BUZZIE   KATE   ELLIOTT JR.

F.D.R.'s children tended to marry young and to reproduce often. By decade's end the record was: seven marriages, two divorces, nine youngsters.

Something Old, Something New

I'm established now for '38

With the title of glamor and reprobate.

I've won a position in Vogue and Harper's;

For a hundred bucks I'll advertise garters.

I grit my teeth and smile at my enemies;

I sit at the Stork Club and talk to nonentities.

"GLAMOR GIRL SERENADE" BY BRENDA FRAZIER, 1938

When most of the country hit rock bottom, old-fashioned High Society foundered along with it. Out of the rubble of Newport and Fifth Avenue, however, emerged some survivors who joined a pack of movie stars and gossip columnists and various hangers-on to create something new: a glittering, publicity-mad, indefatigable set called "Café Society." The "cafés" where this group sported were the old speak-easies, which after Prohibition was repealed in 1933 were reborn as chic restaurants: New York's Stork Club, El Morocco, "21," and the like.

The queen of the new gentlefolk was Brenda Frazier, heiress granddaughter of social arbiter Lady Williams-Taylor and so-called Glamor Girl of 1938. On any given night Brenda might be seen dining with her latest beau at the Colony. On such an evening, the table next to Brenda's would be presided over by someone like Grand Duchess Marie, cousin to Russia's last czar and now a commercial photographer. The Duchess, a formidable presence in her own right, usually appeared with a clutch of other deposed Europeans: Prince Serge Obolensky, who ran a restaurant at the St. Regis Hotel; and Princess Ketto Mikeladze, the negligée buyer at Elizabeth Arden's. Occasionally the expatriate crowd would admit into their

presence their dear friend, red-hot mama Sophie Tucker.

Such egalitarianism was typical of the new free-for-all, in which Astors, Vanderbilts and Whitneys mixed with popular entertainers, while English titleholders sipped cocktails with advertising executives. Marrying and divorcing were equally indiscriminate: women bore names such as "Mrs. Margaret Emerson-McKim-Vanderbilt-Baker-Amory-Emerson" and "Mrs. Millicent Rogers-Salm-Hoogstraetan-Ramos-Balcom."

The ring-mistress of it all was Elsa Maxwell, a fat nobody from Keokuk, Iowa, who had somehow managed to meet *everybody*. She was also quite adroit at getting instant publicity for favored friends. Thus a socially ambitious new woman in town would wangle an invitation to one of Elsa's bashes. And if that same woman had a good press agent, she might finally win one of Café Society's ultimate accolades—her picture in the new picture magazine LIFE with a caption like the following classic tribute to conspicuous inconsequence: "Mrs. Orson D. Munn, who won fame in a limited circle by wearing a foxtail for a hat at the Colony Restaurant, drops in at El Morocco several times a week, is known for the spirited way she dances the rumba with her remarkably agile husband."

Shouting "Oy!" two dancers do the final step of the Lambeth Walk, which originated in England in 1938 and was adopted by Americans.

With suave smile and drooping lids, Alfred G. Vanderbilt dances with film star Joan Crawford at the 1937 Screen Actors Guild Ball in Los Angeles.

A light drinker, Vanderbilt has a Coke with starlet K. T. Stevens.   *His Saratoga visit with divorced star Joan Bennett stirs gossip.*

Alfred dates actress known as Margo . . .   pretty torch singer Gertrude Niesen . . .   and Manhattan deb Eleanor Young.

Prince of the Glamor Boys

The male counterpart to the Glamor Girl in Café Society was the Man About Town, and for several seasons Alfred Gwynne Vanderbilt led the pack. He had all the qualifications. He was young and handsome, possessed an old name and had inherited millions. When he was 21 (in 1933) he had also inherited his mother's racing stable, Sagamore Farm, and in 1936 his horses earned more money than those of any other American sportsman. As if all those qualifications weren't enough, Alf had as his half-sister Glamor Girl Mimi Baker. Moreover, he had been elected best-dressed man in America by a group of tailors and he was very clever at holding the tablecloth when Ernest Hemingway wanted to play bull to Alf's *torero*. Almost every night he could be seen night-clubbing with a different Glamor Girl or movie star and he never shooed photographers away or bothered to deny gossip columnist rumors that a "romance was brewing." Then, in 1938, he climaxed his gay career as glamor boy and brought an end to all the romantic rumors by marrying another wealthy race-track addict, Manuela (Molly) Hudson.

Barbara Hutton in 1930

Poor Little Rich Girl

The star-crossed darling of Café Society was Barbara Hutton, an heiress to a $45 million share of the Woolworth fortune. When she was 13, she wrote prophetically: "Why should some have all / And others be without? / Why should men pretend / And women have to doubt?"

The first man to pretend he loved Barbara, and whom she learned to doubt too late, was a self-styled Russian prince, Alexis Mdivani. Mdivani first met Barbara on the Riviera when she was a fat, homely teenager. Although he was honeymooning with his first bride, American heiress Louise Van Alen, Mdivani made a beeline for Barbara and chatted with her all afternoon.

After restraining himself for all of three years while Barbara grew up a little, Mdivani demanded and got a million-dollar settlement out of his first wife. Then the good Prince Alexis moved in for the kill. Barbara's thoroughly alarmed father spirited her off on a world tour; but the intrepid Mdivani pursued her to Bangkok, and in a few weeks the happy couple announced their engagement.

The wedding took place in Paris. Barbara presented the Prince with a string of polo ponies and the Prince presented Barbara with a string of jade beads, which she paid for. Barbara's father gave the groom a token million and the newlyweds took off for India. Soon after the honeymoon, however, Mdivani was reported to have screamed at Barbara, "You're as fat as a pig," and to be devoting most of his time to women more svelte. Barbara endured

1933. Barbara Hutton marries Prince Mdivani in Paris.

1934. Barbara returns to America dieted down 44 pounds.

1935. She marries Count von Haugwitz-Reventlow.

1936. Kurt, Barbara baptize their son Lance in London.

1937. Barbara and Kurt (left) admit they will split.

Barbara Hutton in 1940

two subsequent years of neglect and strenuous dieting, but then called it quits and gave Mdivani another two million toward settlement.

A new European aristocrat was lying in wait, Count Kurt von Haugwitz-Reventlow, and the day after she had stopped being a Georgian princess, Barbara became a Danish countess. "Now at last I have found happiness," Barbara announced. "My search is ended. I know that this is safe and sure." Safe and sure it wasn't, but Bar-

---

In a foreign land is a very young woman—only 26—who has had a strange life. She is alone, attacked by her husband. She's an American girl fighting alone across the sea. She's made mistakes, been a silly, wild, foolish girl, given in to temptations—but she's still our own. COLUMNIST ADELA ROGERS ST. JOHNS, 1938.

---

bara spared no expense in trying to make it so. For one thing, she shelled out $4.5 million building a huge mansion in London. During her stay in England, Barbara gave birth to her only child, Lance. A year later, in 1937, the marriage was on the rocks and Barbara commented: "Poor Kurt, I feel sorry for him. It was always, 'I am Count von Haugwitz-Reventlow.' He never forgot it—until one day I said, 'Who cares? Who cares about the Count von Haugwitz-Reventlow today? The world has come a long way from that sort of thing.'"

The world had also come a long way from admiring flighty heiresses. In 1939, when Barbara returned to the U.S., Woolworth clerks picketed her hotel and crowds threatened her. "Why do they hate me?" Barbara asked. "There are other girls as rich, richer, almost as rich."

Labor

Cleveland cops move in as strikers overturn a foreman's car.

The Worker Finds a Voice

Labor, like Israel, has many sorrows. Its women keep their fallen and they lament for the future of the children of the race.

JOHN L. LEWIS

By the middle of the 1930s the American workingman was stalking toward a deadly showdown with management. Thanks largely to the shrewd lobbying of bushy-browed John L. Lewis, formidable leader of the United Mine Workers, a federal law was on the books guaranteeing every laborer the right to join a union and use the union to bargain with his bosses. But acknowledging labor's rights by law was easier said than done. In many a big industrial town the only real law was the company's.

In those harsh times, firing was about the mildest punishment given a union organizer. A fair number of U.S. laborers actually worked at gunpoint. Why, a Senate committee had wanted to know in 1928, did the Pittsburgh Coal Company keep machine guns at its coal pits? "You cannot run the mines without them," replied Richard B. Mellon, chairman of the board. In 1935 hired guns still loomed over the toughest of the company towns, where a word for the union could get a man beaten up or killed.

When a strike was brewing in 1935 against the Akron, Ohio, tire manufacturers, the rubber companies had an army of strikebreakers standing by under the direction of one Pearl Bergoff, a king among strikebreakers. Pearl's delicate name mocked his nature (his mother gave him

the name she had picked for the daughter she wanted to have). He ran a multi-million-dollar business, serving various major firms across the country, from an office in New York. His aides daily scanned out-of-town newspapers for hints of brewing strikes, whereupon Pearl dispatched one of his salesmen to peddle the Bergoff services. The deal included shipping a small army of men to fill the struck jobs and fitting them out with weapons from Pearl's armory of machine guns, night sticks and tear gas.

Bergoff was not the only big-time goon for hire. The Pinkerton National Detective Agency, a favorite of the auto companies, earned $1,750,000 for its services to industry between 1933 and 1936. "We must do it," explained Vice President Herman L. Weckler of the Chrysler Corporation, "to obtain the information we need in dealing with our employees." By the mid '30s, however, industrial employees all over the country had long since become fed up with such dealing. And they were rallying behind John L. Lewis, whose tough leadership and political power had brought a new era into view.

They could hardly have had a better man. Lewis had been in the thick of union wars for 25 years. As a teenager with a seventh-grade education, he had gone to work

In 1936, labor czar John L. Lewis blasts Republican Presidential candidate Alf Landon as a "pitiful puppet responsible to the steel industry."

in the coal pits of Iowa with his five kid brothers. His awesome energies, angry convictions and eloquent tongue soon won him a niche of his own in the United Mine Workers. A six-foot-three-inch bull of a man, Lewis had a mind as powerful as his imposing physique. At night and on union organizing trips across the country, he read in their entirety the Bible, the Odyssey and the Iliad, Oswald Spengler and Shakespeare, Karl Marx and Friedrich Engels. By early 1934 this unique mixture of coal miner, labor organizer and reader of classics was entrenched as president of the UMW, and with the backing of the new federal law, he had built the union to 400,000 members and taken the field against intransigent mine owners of Pennsylvania in the first of the decade's climactic labor wars. This occurred in midsummer of 1934, when Lewis called out 70,000 miners to strike.

The companies and their political allies girded for battle. "We're going to meet 'em at the bridge and break their goddam heads," shouted the mayor of Duquesne as the strike spread across the Allegheny Valley. Before it ended, the mine owners had poured some $17,000 into munitions and their henchmen had bombed miners' houses and set crosses ablaze on the hillsides. But in the set-

---

So I'm a Red? I suppose it makes me a Red because I don't like making time so hard on these goddamned machines. When I get home I'm so tired I can't sleep with my wife.

ASSEMBLY-LINE WORKER, 1935

---

tlement, the embattled miners won grudging acceptance, and the road toward union recognition was staked out for every man in America's far-flung laboring forces.

With this triumph under his belt, Lewis met with union organizers in Atlantic City, New Jersey, and proposed a drive to pull together all of the country's industrial laborers into an enormous conglomerate. At one point in the maneuvering, Lewis was challenged by a burly trade unionist who called Lewis a "big bastard," to which Lewis replied with a punch in the nose. When the dust of the skirmish had cleared away, a good many of labor's top

Armed with billy clubs and auto parts, Chrysler strikers rally beneath a slogan—borrowed from French soldiers—warning scabs to stay away.

Sit-down strikers take it easy on assembly-line auto seats inside besieged Fisher Body plant in Flint, Michigan, during the crucial strike of 1937.

men had fallen in behind Lewis; the labor conglomerate was formed and subsequently christened the Congress of Industrial Organizations, the CIO. Looking back with a certain pleasure on the imbroglios involved, Lewis crowed: "They smote me hip and thigh, and right merrily did I return their blows."

Then he returned to the war with industrial management, this time in Flint, Michigan, home of several General Motors plants. General Motors was then the third largest corporation in the country. It employed a quarter of a million people, paying its top 20 officials an average of $200,000, its workers scarcely $1,000. It also maintained one of the rankest spy systems in the country; between January 1934 and August 1936 the company paid $994,855.68 to Pinkerton and others.

On December 28, 1936, a thousand workers at one of GM's Cleveland plants, demanding the right to make every GM worker a member of the United Auto Workers, adopted a somewhat new and disconcertingly effective tactic. They laid down their tools and went on a sit-down strike; instead of walking out, as most earlier strikers had done, they remained in the plant. Management was stunned. Two days later the night shift at GM's key Chevrolet plant in Flint sat down too. Fifteen more plants followed, stripping General Motors of 140,000 employees, and bringing all auto production to a halt.

The focal point of the conflict was at Flint. As the sit-down continued, the temperature dropped below zero, and General Motors officials turned off the heat in the plant and directed the Flint police to seize food bound for the shivering strikers. Some 50 policemen sprayed the pickets with buckshot and tear gas and beat them with clubs. "We wanted peace. General Motors chose war. Give it to them!" shouted a voice over a loudspeaker, and the strikers did, with pipes, door hinges, coffee mugs, pop bottles, and an icy blast from the company's fire hose. After an all-night battle in which 14 men were wounded, the strikers succeeded in routing the police.

Governor Frank Murphy, who had given grueling hours to patient mediation and was determined to keep Mich-

Ford goons stalk unionists Walter Reuther, Richard Frankensteen.

Grabbing Frankensteen, they slug him for handing out union leaflets.

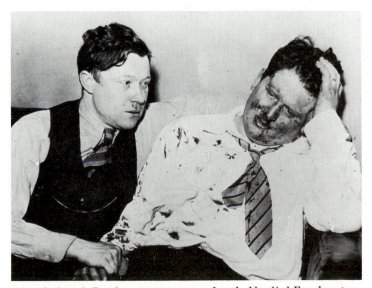

After the brawl, Reuther attempts to comfort the bloodied Frankensteen.

As news of the strikers' victory comes, a jubilant Ladies Auxiliary parades in front of the Chrysler works just before the sit-downers emerge.

igan from further bloodshed, alerted the National Guard. But he decided to consult with Lewis before sending the men into action. What would Lewis do if the Guard tried to evict the strikers, Murphy wanted to know.

"You want my answer, sir?" asked Lewis. "I give it to you. Tomorrow morning, I shall personally enter General Motors plant Chevrolet No. 4. I shall order the men to disregard your order. I shall then walk up to the largest window in the plant, open it, divest myself of my outer raiment, remove my shirt and bare my bosom. Then when you order your troops to fire, mine will be the first those bullets will strike. And as my body falls from that window to the ground, you listen to the voice of your grandfather as he whispers in your ear, 'Frank, are you sure you are doing the right thing?' " Murphy, whose grandfather had been hanged in the Irish rebellion, blanched and tore up his order. He further forbade General Motors to bar the delivery of food to the strikers and with great tact held further violence at bay.

After 44 days of losing profits at the rate of one million dollars a day, General Motors capitulated, agreeing to bargain with the United Automobile Workers in the 17 plants that had been struck. In four months' time the U.A.W. had won its drive for acceptance and organized a majority of General Motors workers. The strikers had scored a monumental triumph against the third mightiest corporation in the country. In the wake of that victory labor's final battles for union recognition got under way.

When they tie the can to a union man,
    Sit down! Sit down!
When they give him the sack they'll take him back,
    Sit down! Sit down!
When the speed-up comes, just twiddle your thumbs,
    Sit down! Sit down!
When the boss won't talk, don't take a walk,
    Sit down! Sit down!

UNION BALLAD

After a Saturday matinee, kids hug their door prizes.

Slinky Jean Harlow gazes longingly at herself in "Dinner at Eight." Called the "Blonde Bombshell," she was the sexiest siren of the early '30s.

Sexiest male, by popular acclaim, was Clark Gable, shown here in his costume for the part of Mr. Christian in "Mutiny on the Bounty."

JEZEBEL

MARKED WOMAN

The Versatile Vixen

Very likely the most talented star of the decade was a popeyed little dynamo named Bette Davis. Though her own personality was so strong that every screen character she played, from *The Old Maid* to *Jezebel*, was unmistakably Bette Davis, she was nevertheless able to inject a biting realism into a remarkable range of roles. Off-screen she was every bit as strong-willed and sharp-tongued as the characters she played in her films. Her leading man Errol Flynn once commented to her, "I'd love to proposition you, Bette, but I'm afraid you'd laugh at me." Bette responded sweetly, "You're so right, Errol."

PETRIFIED FOREST

OF HUMAN BONDAGE

DARK VICTORY

JUAREZ

THE OLD MAID

Errol Flynn leers at the Virgin Queen in "The Private Lives of Elizabeth and Essex," in which Bette Davis played the 60-year-old monarch.

Fiddling fairies swirl in "Gold Diggers of 1933." This sequence is typical of the choreography of Busby Berkeley, master of '30s musicals.

Swing

Two swing musicians get top billing on a Broadway marquee.

The Leaders

Big bands became big business in the late '30s and their leaders were as famous as movie stars. In fact, many band leaders made full-length movies. Benny Goodman appeared in *The Big Broadcast of 1937;* Bob Crosby was featured in *Let's Make Music.* As with other celebrities, lives of the big-band leaders became fair game for gossip-mongers. When the hot-tempered musical brothers Tommy and Jimmy Dorsey feuded over the proper tempo for a song in 1935 and split up the Dorsey Brothers Orchestra, the story was big news. Another hot item was the marriage of bandleader Kay Kyser to his svelte blonde vocalist, Georgia Carroll. Equally well-known among musicians and fans was the notorious Goodman "ray," or stare; Benny Goodman was a perfectionist, and if he turned his "ray" on an underrehearsed musician, the man's days with the band were considered numbered.

The most dedicated swing fans followed the exploits of their heroes in *Downbeat* and *Metronome,* the trade journals of the popular band musicians. Every year both magazines asked readers to write in the names of their favorite bands. The two polls made a distinction between "sweet" bands, which played the schmaltzy sound popularized by the likes of Guy Lombardo, and swing bands, those with a hard-driving beat and improvised solos. The men at right were the top 10 swing band leaders of 1939 as selected in *Metronome.*

1. Benny Goodman

"Metronome's" top band leader, the clarinet-playing Goodman was celebrated as "The King of Swing."

2. Artie Shaw

Shaw, though not as hot a clarinetist as Goodman, had a band many fans rated as swinging as Benny's.

3. Tommy Dorsey

After breaking with his brother Jimmy, trombonist Tommy created a new band with a brassier sound.

4. Bob Crosby

Bing's kid brother, Bob Crosby, sang with the Dorseys before he left to lead a popular Dixieland band.

5. Glenn Miller

An excellent arranger, trombonist Glenn Miller played music noted for fast tempos and lead clarinets.

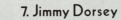

7. Jimmy Dorsey

Playing both alto sax and clarinet, Jimmy wavered between Dixieland and the more modern swing sound.

9. Jimmie Lunceford

Lunceford's group was one of the decade's most dynamic bands, with its showmanship and bouncy beat.

6. Count Basie

Basie's 15-man band featured great vocalists like Jimmy Rushing and the Count's own droll piano style.

8. Harry James

At first a trumpet soloist with Goodman, James started his own group in 1939—with Benny's backing.

10. Duke Ellington

A gifted composer, the Duke created a sophisticated style using a jazz sound he called "jungle music."

Martha Tilton

Known as "Liltin' Martha Tilton," she made "And the Angels Sing" a hit record in 1939 with Benny Goodman.

Helen O'Connell

Famous as Jimmy Dorsey's canary, swing fans voted her the top female vocalist of 1940, when she was twenty.

Billie Holiday

The great jazz vocalist Billie Holiday was almost unknown when she joined the Artie Shaw Orchestra in 1938.

Canaries and Hits

Almost all the big bands, swing and sweet alike, featured vocalists, usually female. The hot voices—or cool looks—of these singers (*aficionados* called them canaries) often outdid the orchestras in putting across hit tunes. Above is a lineup of canaries of the late '30s and at right are box scores from the entertainment newspaper *Variety* of the top 15 tunes from 1936 to 1940. As the charts show, many of the most popular songs of the swing age were not strictly swing.

1936

ALL MY EGGS IN ONE BASKET
ALONE
CHAPEL IN THE MOONLIGHT
DID I REMEMBER?
IS IT TRUE WHAT THEY SAY ABOUT DIXIE?
IT'S A SIN TO TELL A LIE
LIGHTS OUT
MOON OVER MIAMI
THE MUSIC GOES 'ROUND AND 'ROUND
ON THE BEACH AT BALI BALI
PENNIES FROM HEAVEN
RED SAILS IN THE SUNSET
THE WAY YOU LOOK TONIGHT
WHEN DID YOU LEAVE HEAVEN?
WHEN I'M WITH YOU

1937

BOO HOO
CHAPEL IN THE MOONLIGHT
HARBOR LIGHTS
IT LOOKS LIKE RAIN
LITTLE OLD LADY
MOONLIGHT AND SHADOWS
MY CABIN OF DREAMS
ONCE IN A WHILE
SAILBOAT IN THE MOONLIGHT
SEPTEMBER IN THE RAIN
SO RARE
THAT OLD FEELING
VIENI VIENI
WHEN MY DREAMBOAT COMES HOME
YOU CAN'T STOP ME FROM DREAMING

Mildred Bailey

Singing ballads such as "Willow Weep for Me," Mildred was the top attraction for her husband Red Norvo's band.

Marion Hutton

Blonde Marion Hutton was a vocalist for Glenn Miller. At this time her sister, Betty Hutton, was also a singer.

Ella Fitzgerald

Discovered in an amateur show at age 17, Ella joined Chick Webb and dazzled fans with "A-Tisket A-Tasket."

1938

ALEXANDER'S RAGTIME BAND

A-TISKET A-TASKET

BEI MIR BIST DU SCHÖN

CATHEDRAL IN THE PINES

HEIGH-HO

I'VE GOT A POCKETFUL OF DREAMS

LOVE WALKED IN

MUSIC, MAESTRO, PLEASE!

MY REVERIE

ROSALIE

SAYS MY HEART

THANKS FOR THE MEMORY

THERE'S A GOLD MINE IN THE SKY

TI-PI-TIN

WHISTLE WHILE YOU WORK

1939

AND THE ANGELS SING

BEER BARREL POLKA

DEEP IN A DREAM

DEEP PURPLE

JEEPERS CREEPERS

MAN WITH THE MANDOLIN

MOON LOVE

MY PRAYER

OVER THE RAINBOW

PENNY SERENADE

SUNRISE SERENADE

THREE LITTLE FISHIES

UMBRELLA MAN

WISHING

YOU MUST HAVE BEEN A BEAUTIFUL BABY

1940

BLUEBERRY HILL

CARELESS

FERRYBOAT SERENADE

GOD BLESS AMERICA

I'LL NEVER SMILE AGAIN

IN AN OLD DUTCH GARDEN

INDIAN SUMMER

MAKE BELIEVE ISLAND

OH JOHNNY

ONLY FOREVER

PLAYMATES

SCATTERBRAIN

SOUTH OF THE BORDER

WHEN YOU WISH UPON A STAR

WOODPECKER SONG

Merry Days at Mad Meadow

Here is the magnificent spectacle of a luminous world, apparently suspended in space . . .

OFFICIAL FAIR GUIDE BOOK

. . . and your fellow fairgoers trudge on numbed feet with dazed eyes.

LIFE, JULY 3, 1939

The New York World's Fair was the biggest, giddiest, costliest and most ambitious international exposition ever put on. Even before it opened, on April 30, 1939, amid a blaze of fireworks and a blast of windy publicity, it had cost more than $150 million. Its 1,216-acre grounds in Flushing Meadow, Queens, had been made to order by filling in the entire Queens city dump and planting it with 10,000 trees and one million tulips from Holland. Upon this tract had been built 300 massive, futuristic buildings to house the Fair's 1,500 exhibitors. They included 33 states, 58 foreign countries and 1,300 business firms, ranging from the Ford Motor Company to Dr. Scholl's Footease, which maintained an emergency clinic to treat fairgoers whose arches had sagged along the exposition's 65 miles of paved streets and footpaths.

The Fair's president, gardenia-wearing Grover Aloysius Whalen, had christened this gigantic conglomeration "The World of Tomorrow" and dedicated it to both the blessings of democracy and the wonders of technology. The latter included such marvels as television, nylon stockings, a robot named Elektro that could talk and puff a cigarette, nude statues with titles like Freedom of Assembly, and at the Fair's Theme Centre, the 700-foot-tall needlelike Trylon and the 200-foot globe called the Perisphere.

Mixed in with the technological marvels, the Fair's 45 million visitors found a bewildering assortment of promotional gimmicks, side shows and downright corn, which prompted *The New York Times's* Meyer Berger to refer to the Fair as "Mad Meadow." "See me get milked on a merry-go-round!" shouted the poster hawking Elsie, the Borden Cow, and sure enough, at the Borden exhibit you could see 150 of Elsie's sisters being spun on a revolving milking platform. If you were unlucky, you might hit Elsie on her birthday and hear a squad of Western Union boys deliver a singing telegram: "Mooey Birthday to You." At Ford there was a floor show entitled "A Thousand Times Neigh," a horse's-eye view of the automobile, and Life Savers offered a sky dive *(opposite)*. You could even take in a skin show and ogle an innocent (nearly nude) maiden as she wrestled with Oscar the Obscene Octopus in "Twenty Thousand Legs Under the Sea."

In its two-year run, in fact, the Fair provided just about everything for everybody. "It was the paradox of all paradoxes," wrote Sidney M. Shalett in *Harper's* magazine in 1940. "It was good, it was bad; it was the acme of all crazy vulgarity, it was the pinnacle of all inspiration."

High point of the Fair's Amusement Area was the 250-foot parachute jump, which in two years thrilled two million riders.

Picture Credits

The sources for the illustrations which appear in this book are shown here. Credits for the pictures from left to right are separated by semicolons, from top to bottom by dashes.

Cover—Underwood and Underwood/The Bettmann Archive.

2,3—Historical Collection Security Pacific National Bank. 4,5—Culver Pictures. 6—Culver Pictures. 7—Irving Settel; John Phillips; Culver Pictures. 8,9—Special Collections Division, University of Washington Libraries, Photo by James Lee, Negative No.: 20102. 10—*The Detroit News.* 11—Library of Congress. 12,13—Library of Congress. 14,15—Library of Congress. 16,17—Library of Congress. 19—The Archives of Labor and Urban Affairs, Wayne State University. 20—Chicago Tribune-New York News Syndicate courtesy Woody Gelman and Nostalgia Press. 21—John Savage courtesy Ernest Trova except bottom left courtesy Woody Gelman. 22—John Savage courtesy Ernest Trova except bottom left courtesy Ernest Trova and Ralston Purina Co. 23—John Savage courtesy Ernest Trova. 25—No credit. 26—UPI/Bettmann Newsphotos except top left *Oklahoman.* 27—Charles Moore from Black Star. 29—Courtesy Vanity Fair. Copyright © 1934 (renewed 1962) by the Condé Nast Publications, Inc. 30—Underwood and Underwood/The Bettmann Archive. 31—UPI/Bettmann Newsphotos except second from right Wide World—*The New York Times* and Wide World courtesy Franklin D. Roosevelt Library, Hyde Park, New York; UPI/Bettmann Newsphotos; Wide World (2); Keystone View; Wide World; Arthur Griffin—UPI/Bettmann Newsphotos; Wide World; no credit; UPI/Bettmann Newsphotos; Wide World; UPI/Bettmann Newsphotos—UPI/Bettmann Newsphotos; Wide World; Franklin D. Roosevelt Library, Hyde Park, New York. 33—UPI/Bettmann Newsphotos. 34—UPI/Bettmann Newsphotos. 35—Photo World (Edward Ozern); Culver Pictures—Stork Club; Wide World; Jerome Zerbe. 36—Wide World; Underwood and Underwood/The Bettmann Archive—Wide World—UPI/Bettmann Newsphotos. 37—Underwood and Underwood/The Bettmann Archive except top right UPI/Bettmann Newsphotos. 38,39—Interphoto. 41—Phototrends. 42,43—The Archives of Labor and Urban Affairs, Wayne State University. 44—Library of Congress. 45—Wide World except bottom UPI/Bettmann Newsphotos. 46,47—The Archives of Labor and Urban Affairs, Wayne State University. 48,49—San Diego Historical Society. 50,51—Culver Pictures. 52—Courtesy Culver Pictures, Copyright Turner Entertainment Co.; Courtesy Photo Files, Copyright Turner Entertainment Co.—Courtesy Photo Files, Copyright Turner Entertainment Co.; Courtesy Culver Pictures, Copyright Turner Entertainment Co.—Courtesy Academy of Motion Picture Arts and Sciences, Copyright Turner Entertainment Co.; Courtesy Culver Pictures, Copyright Turner Entertainment Co.; Courtesy Warner Bros., Copyright Turner Entertainment Co. 53—Courtesy Warner Bros., Copyright Turner Entertainment Co. 54,55—Brown Brothers. 56,57—Popsie, New York. 58—No credit—Brown Brothers; Ernest R. Smith—The Bettmann Archive. 59—Reprinted with permission of *Down Beat* magazine; Brown Brothers; Photo Files; Duncan P. Schiedt; Photo Files. 60,61—Popsie, New York except left reprinted with permission of *Down Beat* magazine. 63—Frank T. Sobeck.

Text Credits

10—Auto worker quote adapted from *The New Republic,* March 18, 1931, pp. 118-119. 21—"Little Orphan Annie Song" courtesy of Ovaltine Food Products.